CLB 2632
© 1991 Colour Library Books Ltd., Godalming, Surrey, England.
All rights reserved
This edition published 1991 by Gallery Books,
an imprint of W.H Smith Publishers, Inc,
112 Madison Avenue, New York 10016
Colour separations by Hong Kong Graphic Arts Ltd., Hong Kong
Printed and bound in Singapore by Tien Wah Press (PTE) Ltd.,
ISBN 0 8317 5987 9

Gallery Books are available for bulk purchase for sales promotions
and premium use. For details write or telephone
the Manager of Special Sales, WH Smith Publishers, Inc,
12 Madison Avenue, New York, New York 10016 (212) 532-6600

Microwave
Hot`n`Spicy

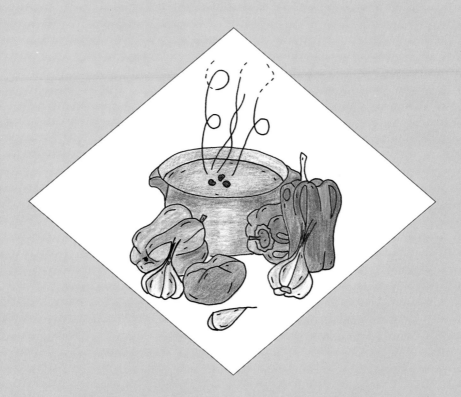

GALLERY BOOKS

An Imprint of W. H. Smith Publishers Inc.
112 Madison Avenue
New York City 10016

Microwave Hot`n´Spicy

Hot and spicy food is popular the world over. Spices stimulate and excite the appetite and, surprisingly, are also said to aid digestion! Microwave ovens are perfect for cooking spicy foods because they bring out the flavor of the food so well. Spices also give excellent color to microwaved food, which may otherwise look bland.

As you might imagine, the range of hot and spicy foods is enormous, so we've gathered together a selection of thirty recipes from around the world: Indian, Chinese, Spanish and Mexican cuisines are well represented, together with recipes from the American Southwest and Bayou country.

Besides their aromatic spiciness, these recipes have one other thing in common: they are all designed to be cooked, quick as a flash, in your microwave oven.

All microwave recipes were prepared in a 700 watt oven. If your microwave is of a lower output, adjust timings as follows:

500 watt – add 40 seconds for every minute stated in the recipe
600 watt – add 20 seconds for every minute stated in the recipe
650 watt – only a slight increase in the overall time is necessary

CALAMARES ESPAÑA

SERVES 4

*The sweet, rich taste of squid blends perfectly with zesty orange,
tomato and chili in this Spanish-style appetizer.*

2 medium-sized squid
1 bay leaf
1 small onion, finely chopped
2 tbsps olive oil
1 clove garlic, finely chopped
2 tbsps flour
8oz canned plum tomatoes
1 chili pepper, seeded and finely chopped
Grated rind and juice of ½ orange
½ cup white wine
1 tbsp tomato paste
1 tsp oregano
1 tsp basil
Salt and pepper
Fresh coriander leaves to garnish

Step 1 Separate the head and tail of each squid and remove the ink sac and quill.

1. Separate heads of the squid from the tails. Remove the ink sac and reserve for the sauce if desired. Remove the quill and discard.

2. Cut the tentacles above the eyes, and reserve. Discard the eyes and head.

3. Peel the purplish membrane off the tail portion of the squid. Split the tail in half, lengthwise, and wash it well. Cut the tail into pieces about 2 inches wide.

4. Score each section in a lattice pattern at ¼-inch intervals. Separate the tentacles.

5. Put the squid, bay leaf and onion into a casserole with hot water. Cover loosely and cook for 1 minute on HIGH.

6. Heat the olive oil for 30 seconds on HIGH in a medium-sized bowl. Add the garlic and cook for a further 1 minute on HIGH.

7. Stir in the flour. Mix in the cooking liquid from the squid together with the tomatoes and remaining

Step 5 Cook the squid, bay leaf and onion in water until squid is tender and begins to curl.

sauce ingredients. If using the ink, break the ink sac into the sauce ingredients.

8. Cook the sauce, uncovered, for 5 minutes on HIGH. Mix with the squid and serve garnished with fresh coriander leaves.

Cook's Notes

TIME: Preparation takes about 20 minutes, and cooking takes about 8 minutes.

SERVING IDEAS: This can be served either hot or cold, as a starter for 4 or a main course for 2 people, with pasta or rice.

WATCHPOINT: When cooking seafood of any kind in a microwave oven, watch it carefully to be sure it does not overcook and become tough. Squid cook especially fast and will begin to pop if overcooked.

TACOS VERACRUZ
SERVES 4

The seafood "cousin" of the beef taco is every bit as spicy and every bit as much fun to put together and to eat.

Topping
1 ripe avocado, peeled and mashed
2 tomatoes, seeded and chopped
1 small clove garlic, crushed
1 tbsp lime or lemon juice

Filling
1 tbsp oil
1 shallot, finely chopped
½ green pepper, chopped
1 tsp ground cumin
½ red or green chili pepper, seeded and finely
    chopped
4 tbsps tomato paste
6 tbsps water
Salt and pepper
¾ cup cooked, peeled shrimp, roughly chopped

4 taco shells

1. First mix the topping ingredients together, cover and set aside.

2. Heat the oil in a small, deep bowl for 30 seconds on HIGH. Add the shallot, green pepper, cumin and chili pepper and cook for 2-3 minutes to soften slightly. Stir once or twice during cooking.

3. Add the tomato paste and water. If the sauce is too thick add an additional spoonful of water.

4. Add the salt and pepper and stir in the shrimp. Cook for 2-3 minutes on MEDIUM to heat the shrimp through.

5. Spoon into the taco shells and top with the avocado mixture.

Step 1 Mix the topping ingredients together, mashing the avocado into small pieces. The mixture should not be smooth.

Step 2 Soften the shallot and green pepper in the oil before adding the remaining sauce ingredients.

Step 5 Spoon the filling and topping into open taco shells.

Cook's Notes

TIME: Preparation takes about 15 minutes, and cooking takes about 6 minutes.

COOK'S TIP: When heating taco shells in a microwave oven, stand them on their open ends. This keeps them from closing up.

 VARIATION: Use crabmeat in place of the shrimp.

CHILI SHRIMP

SERVES 4

*For a spicy, spirited start to an oriental feast, these shrimp are quick
and easy and full of flavor.*

1lb large shrimp
2 tbsps oil
2 cloves garlic, crushed
2 tbsps chili sauce (hot or sweet)
1 tbsp rice wine
1 tbsp lemon juice
Salt

1. Remove the heads and shells of the shrimp, but leave on the very ends of the tails. Wash, devein and pat dry.

2. Put the oil and garlic into a bowl and cover with plastic wrap. Cook on HIGH for 1 minute.

3. Stir in the chili sauce, wine, lemon juice and salt. Cook for 30 seconds on HIGH.

4. Add the shrimp and cook for 3-4 minutes on MEDIUM.

Step 1 Shell the shrimp, removing their heads but leaving the tails intact.

Step 4 Add the shrimp to the oil and garlic and stir well before cooking further.

Cook's Notes

TIME: Preparation takes about 10-15 minutes, and cooking takes 4-5 minutes.

VARIATION: If uncooked shrimp are not available, use cooked shrimp and cut the cooking time by half.

SERVING IDEAS: As an appetizer these may be served hot or cold. Chili pepper flowers make an attractive garnish, but are not to be eaten. To make them, cut chili pepper in thin strips from the pointed end to the stem end, but not completely through the stem. Rinse out the seeds and leave pepper in iced water for several hours. The strips will open up like petals.

PORK SATAY WITH PEANUT SAUCE

SERVES 4

*Fragrant spices and hot chilies are characteristic ingredients in
Indonesian food such as this delicious appetizer.*

Juice of 2 limes
Salt and pepper
1½lbs pork tenderloin, cut into 1-inch cubes
1 large red pepper, cut into 1-inch pieces
2 tbsps oil
1 shallot, finely chopped
1 small green chili pepper, seeded and finely
   chopped
½ cup chicken or vegetable stock
1 tsp cornstarch
½ cup crunchy peanut butter
1 clove garlic, crushed
1 tsp ground cumin
1 tsp ground coriander
1 bunch fresh coriander leaves, to garnish

Step 3 Add the stock, peanut butter and other sauce ingredients and cook to thicken.

Step 4 Thread the pork and red pepper onto wooden skewers. Do not pack together too tightly.

Step 2 In a small bowl, cook the shallot in the oil before adding the chili pepper.

1. Mix the lime juice, salt and pepper together and mix in the pork and the pepper pieces. Leave in a cool place for 1 hour.

2. Heat 1 tbsp oil in a small bowl and add the shallot. Cook for 2 minutes on HIGH, add the chili pepper and cook for 1 minute more on HIGH.

3. Mix the stock with the cornstarch, and add the peanut butter, spices and seasoning. Cook for 1 minute on HIGH. Set aside.

4. Thread the meat and red pepper onto 12 small, wooden skewers. Heat a browning tray for 5 minutes on HIGH. Add the remaining 1 tbsp oil and brown the satay for 3 minutes on HIGH, turning frequently.

5. Transfer to a roasting rack, and cook for 6 minutes on MEDIUM.

6. Arrange sprigs of coriander leaves on serving plates and put the satay on top. Spoon over some of the peanut sauce and serve the rest separately.

Cook's Notes

TIME: Preparation takes about 10 minutes, plus 1 hour marinating time. Cooking takes about 13 minutes.

PREPARATION: The sauce may be served at room temperature or cooked just before serving. It does not reheat well.

SERVING IDEAS: This appetizer can also be a main course if served with rice.

INDIAN OMELET

MAKES 1

Omelets aren't necessarily French. This recipe shows an Indian influence using sunny tomatoes, pungent coriander and hot chili to add interest to eggs.

1 tbsp butter or margarine
½ onion, finely chopped
1 small tomato, peeled, seeded and chopped
½ green chili, seeded and chopped
1 sprig coriander, chopped
2 eggs, separated
1 tsp water
Salt and pepper

Step 3 Fold the stiffly beaten egg whites gently but thoroughly into the yolks.

Step 1 Cook the onion in the butter and add the tomato, chili and coriander.

Step 4 Spoon the egg mixture into the pie dish and smooth the top.

1. Melt the butter in a shallow pie pan for 30 seconds on HIGH. Cook the onion for 1-2 minutes to soften and add the tomato, chili and coriander.

2. Beat the egg yolks with the water.

3. Beat the egg whites until stiff but not dry and fold into the yolks.

4. Spoon the egg mixture into the pie dish, smoothing the top. Cook for 4 minutes on MEDIUM or until set.

5. Fold over to serve, or turn out of the dish and cut into wedges.

Cook's Notes

TIME: Preparation takes about 10 minutes, and cooking takes 5-6 minutes.

PREPARATION: Microwave omelettes are lighter and fluffier than those cooked conventionally, but they can overcook very quickly, so careful attention is needed.

VARIATION: A spicier omelet can be created by adding cumin or curry powder to the dish while softening the tomato and chili.

SPICY CHICKEN KEBABS WITH AVOCADO SAUCE

SERVES 4

Curry powder makes microwaved chicken more interesting. Avocado sauce provides a wonderful contrast of taste, texture and color.

3 chicken breasts, skinned and boned

Marinade
2 tbsps vegetable oil
1 clove garlic, crushed
1 tbsp curry powder
¼ tsp cayenne pepper
1 tbsp chopped coriander leaves
Juice and grated rind of 1 lime
Salt and pepper

Sauce
1 tbsp vegetable oil
½ tsp finely chopped onion
1 tsp mango chutney
1 large avocado, peeled and stone removed
½ cup plain yogurt
2 tsps lime juice to taste

1. Cut chicken into strips 1 inch wide. Combine ingredients for the marinade and mix in the chicken to coat each piece. Leave to marinate for 1 hour.

2. Thread the meat onto wooden skewers and put onto a roasting rack. Cook for 5 minutes on HIGH.

3. Turn kebabs while cooking. Leave to stand, covered in plastic wrap, for 1 minute.

4. Put the oil and onion for the sauce into a small bowl. Cook for 1 minute on HIGH, and stir in the chutney.

5. Put avocado flesh into a food processor with the seasoning, yogurt and lime juice. Add onion and chutney, and process until smooth. Serve with the chicken kebabs.

Step 1 Cut chicken into strips and marinate in the spice mixture.

Step 2 Thread the meat onto skewers and place on a microwave roasting rack.

Step 3 Turn kebabs and baste frequently with the remaining marinade.

Cook's Notes

TIME: Preparation time takes about 10 minutes, plus 1 hour marinating time, and cooking takes about 6 minutes.

PREPARATION: Depending on your oven, you may want to cook the chicken on a medium setting to prevent the flesh splitting which can occur on high settings.

COOK'S TIP: When preparing sauces with avocado, leave the stone in the mixture until ready to serve. This will help keep the mixture green.

KUNG-PAO LAMB

SERVES 4

_This memorable dish, with its unusual blend of flavors, is named
after a governor of Szechuan, whose official title was "Kung Pao"._

1lb lamb fillet or meat from the leg, thinly sliced
2 tbsps oil
1 clove garlic, finely chopped
1 small piece fresh ginger root, grated
½ red chili pepper, seeded and finely chopped
4 tbsps soy sauce
½ cup stock
2 tbsps white wine
1 tsp vinegar
1 tsp sugar
1 tbsp cornstarch
1 small red pepper, cut in small dice
1 small green pepper, cut in small dice
Dash sesame oil
4 green onions, sliced
½ cup roasted peanuts

Step 3 Blend the soy sauce, stock, wine, vinegar, sugar and cornstarch and mix into the browned meat.

Step 5 Stir in the sesame oil, peanuts and onions for the last 30 seconds of cooking.

Step 1 In a preheated browning dish, cook the lamb in the oil, pressing the meat against the dish to promote browning.

1. Heat a browning dish for 5 minutes on HIGH. Combine the lamb and oil and add to the dish. Cook for about 2 minutes, turning often. Cook in two batches if necessary.

2. Add the garlic, ginger and chili pepper and cook for a further 2 minutes on HIGH.

3. Mix the soy sauce, stock, wine, vinegar, sugar and cornstarch together and add to the meat.

4. Cover the browning dish or transfer the ingredients to a covered casserole dish. Cook on MEDIUM for a further 4-6 minutes or until the lamb is tender.

5. Add the diced peppers and cook for a further 1 minute on HIGH. Stir in the sesame oil, the green onions and peanuts. Heat for 30 seconds on HIGH.

Cook's Notes

 TIME: Preparation takes about 20 minutes, and cooking takes 10-11 minutes.

 VARIATION: Other nuts such as cashews or almonds may be used instead of peanuts.

 SERVING IDEAS: Serve with plain boiled rice or fried rice.

SZECHUAN BEEF

SERVES 4

Szechuan food is the spiciest of all Chinese cuisine. When cooked in a microwave oven, this meal is even faster than a takeout.

1lb rump steak, thinly sliced
2 tbsps oil
½ dried chili pepper, seeded and crushed
4 tbsps soy sauce
½ cup stock
2 tbsps cornstarch
3 sticks celery, finely shredded
1 sweet red pepper, finely shredded

Step 4 Add the celery and red pepper and mix with the meat and sauce.

Step 1 Mix the meat and oil together well before adding to the hot browning dish.

Step 5 Cook for a further 1 minute or until the sauce has thickened and cleared.

1. Heat a browning dish according to the manufacturer's instructions, on HIGH. Combine meat and oil and add to the dish.

2. Cook for 2 minutes on HIGH in 2 or 3 batches. Reheat browning dish for 2 minutes after each batch.

3. Add the crushed chili pepper. Mix the soy sauce

and stock and gradually stir into the cornstarch. Pour over the steak and cook for 2-3 minutes.

4. Add the celery and red pepper and mix together with the meat and sauce.

5. Cook for a further 1 minute on HIGH until the sauce has thickened but the vegetables are still crisp.

Cook's Notes

 TIME: Preparation takes about 20 minutes, and cooking takes 7-10 minutes.

 VARIATION: If dried chili peppers are unavailable, substitute fresh chilies to taste.

! WATCHPOINT: When removing a browning dish from the microwave oven, always use oven gloves to protect hands. Also, always place hot browning dish on a heatproof mat to protect work surfaces.

VINDALOO

SERVES 4-6

A vindaloo is one of the hottest curries and not for the faint-hearted!
Beef or lamb can also be cooked the same way.

1 tbsp oil
3 cloves garlic, crushed
¼ tsp each of ground cumin, coriander, cinnamon,
 cloves, black pepper, ginger
1½ tsps turmeric
1 tsp mustard seed
1lb pork tenderloin, cut into cubes
3 bay leaves
4 tbsps tamarind extract
2 tsps tomato paste
2 tsps sugar
3 tbsps vinegar
Water or stock to moisten
1-2 green chilies, seeded and chopped
Salt
1 tbsp cornstarch mixed with 3 tbsps water or stock
 (optional)

Step 1 Add the crushed garlic, spices and mustard seed to the oil and cook for 1 minute.

1. Heat the oil and add the garlic, spices and mustard seed. Cook for 1 minute on HIGH.

2. Allow to cool and pour over the pork cubes in a shallow dish. Stir to coat and add the bay leaves. Leave to marinate overnight in the refrigerator,

stirring occasionally.

3. Mix the tamarind, tomato paste, sugar and vinegar and pour over the meat.

4. Add water or stock to come a quarter of the way up the meat, and sprinkle over the chilies. Cover

Step 3 Mix together the tamarind extract, tomato paste, vinegar and sugar and pour this over the meat.

Step 4 Add water or stock to come a quarter of the way up the meat.

the dish and cook for 20 minutes on MEDIUM, adding more water or stock if drying out.

5. When the meat is tender, leave the vindaloo to stand for 5 minutes before serving. If desired, the sauce may be thickened with the cornstarch and water or stock. Cook for 2-3 minutes or until clear.

Cook's Notes

 TIME: Preparation takes about 20 minutes, but meat should marinate overnight for full flavor. Cooking takes 23-24 minutes.

 COOK'S TIP: Most meats benefit from the medium range of settings in microwave ovens which means slower cooking but gives a tender result. The meat will still cook in about half the time of conventional cooking.

$ BUYING GUIDE: Tamarind extract is available from Indian groceries and also from delicatessens. Substitute 2 tbsps mango chutney mixed with 2 tbsps lemon juice, if it is unobtainable.

PEPPERCORN LAMB

SERVES 4

A special dish for a special dinner, this can be made hotter with the addition of more green peppercorns.

4 tbsps butter or margarine
1½ lbs lamb fillet or meat from the leg cut into
   ¼-inch slices
2 shallots, finely chopped
3 tbsps flour
1 clove garlic, finely minced
1 tsp ground allspice
1 cup beef stock
1 tsp tomato paste
1 tbsp canned green peppercorns, rinsed and
   drained
2 pimentos cut into thin strips
¼ cup heavy cream
Salt and pepper

3. Cook the shallots and flour to brown slightly.

4. Add the garlic, allspice, stock and tomato paste. Season with salt and pepper and cook for 2-3 minutes on HIGH, until starting to thicken.

5. Add the lamb, cover and cook for 10 minutes on MEDIUM, or until the lamb is tender.

6. Add the peppercorns, pimento and cream and cook for 2 minutes on HIGH. Adjust the seasoning and leave to stand for 2 minutes, covered.

Step 4 Add the garlic, allspice, stock, tomato paste and seasonings and cook until beginning to thicken.

Step 3 Cook the shallots and flour in the browning dish until slightly colored.

Step 6 When lamb is cooked, add the peppercorns, pimento and cream to the sauce.

1. Heat a browning dish according to the manufacturer's instructions on HIGH. Melt the butter for 1 minute on HIGH and add the slices of lamb.
2. Cook for 2 minutes on HIGH, in 2 or 3 batches. Remove the meat and set aside.

Cook's Notes

TIME: Preparation takes about 13 minutes, and cooking takes 21-22 minutes. Allow 2 minutes standing time.

PREPARATION: When using a browning dish, press the meat firmly against the hot surface of the dish for best results.

BUYING GUIDE: Green peppercorns are available bottled in brine or canned. If bottled in brine, peppercorns need to be rinsed.

TACOS

SERVES 4

Enjoy a taste of Mexico in this easily prepared snack. With various colorful toppings to choose from, you can vary the taste to suit yourself.

½lb ground beef
1 small onion, chopped
1 tbsp raisins
1 tbsp pine nuts
1 tbsp corn
2 tsps chili powder
4oz canned tomatoes
Salt and pepper
8 taco shells

Toppings
1 cup grated cheese
½ cup sour cream
4 tomatoes, chopped
½ head lettuce, shredded
1 chopped avocado

Step 3 Spoon off any excess fat from the meat before adding the other ingredients.

Step 4 Spoon the meat mixture into the taco shells and reheat if necessary.

Step 2 Cook the meat in a covered dish, stirring occasionally to break meat into small pieces.

1. Put the beef and onion into a 1 quart casserole. Break the meat up well with a fork.

2. Cover and cook for 4 minutes on HIGH, stirring occasionally to break into small pieces.

3. Drain any fat from the meat and add the raisins, nuts, sweetcorn, chili powder and tomatoes.

4. Cover and cook on MEDIUM for 8 minutes. Adjust seasoning. Spoon into the taco shells and serve with the various toppings.

Cook's Notes

 TIME: Preparation takes about 15 minutes, and cooking takes about 12 minutes.

 BUYING GUIDE: Taco shells are now readily available in supermarkets and delicatessens.

 PREPARATION: Reheat unfilled taco shells by standing them on paper towels on their open ends. This stops shells from closing up.

 VARIATION: Pine nuts, which are expensive, can be replaced with walnuts or almonds or the nuts may be omitted altogether.

MEXICAN PORK CASSEROLE

SERVES 4

All the favorite flavors of Mexican cooking—chickpeas, beans, peppers, chilies and spices—combine with pork in one easy-to-cook casserole.

2 tsps oil
1lb pork tenderloin, cut into 1-inch cubes
¼ tsp ground cumin
¼ tsp ground coriander
1 small onion, chopped
1 clove garlic, crushed
2 tbsps flour
1 tbsp instant coffee
1½ cups stock
½ red pepper, diced
½ green pepper, diced
1 small chili pepper, seeded and chopped
2½ cups canned red kidney beans, rinsed
2½ cups canned chickpeas, rinsed
Tortilla chips to garnish

Step 3 Add the coffee and stock to the casserole, stirring constantly to blend well.

Step 5 Add the beans and chickpeas to the casserole and heat through.

Step 2 Cook the cumin, coriander, garlic, onion and flour for 1-2 minutes.

1. Heat a browning dish for 5 minutes on HIGH. Put in the oil and add the pork cubes. Cook for 4 minutes on HIGH, stirring frequently, until slightly browned.

2. Add the cumin, coriander, garlic, onion and flour, and cook for 1-2 minutes on HIGH.

3. Dissolve the instant coffee in the stock and add to the casserole, stirring well.

4. Add the peppers, cover, and cook on MEDIUM for 30 minutes.

5. Add the beans and chickpeas and heat for 4 minutes on MEDIUM. Serve with tortilla chips.

Cook's Notes

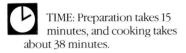 TIME: Preparation takes 15 minutes, and cooking takes about 38 minutes.

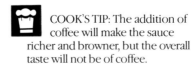 COOK'S TIP: The addition of coffee will make the sauce richer and browner, but the overall taste will not be of coffee.

 VARIATION: Rice may be served instead of the tortilla chips as an accompaniment.

JAMBALAYA

SERVES 4

This classic dish comes from New Orleans in Bayou country.
Whilst the ingredients list looks complicated, the preparation couldn't
be easier.

8oz spicy sausage, such as Pepperoni or Merguez,
   skinned and diced
8oz cooked ham, cubed
1 green pepper, seeded and cut into 1-inch pieces
1 medium onion, roughly chopped
1 clove garlic, finely chopped
1 red or green chili, seeded and finely chopped
2 tbsps olive oil
10oz canned tomatoes
1 tbsp tomato paste
2 tbsps white wine or lemon juice
1 tsp chopped marjoram
1 bay leaf
¼ tsp grated fresh nutmeg
Salt and pepper
4oz peeled, cooked shrimp
2 tomatoes, peeled, seeded and cut into large
   pieces
1½ cups cooked long grain rice

Step 2 Cook the sausage, ham, pepper, onion, garlic and chili until the vegetables are nearly tender.

Step 3 Mix all the remaining ingredients except the tomatoes, rice and shrimp together. Cover the bowl with cling film, piercing it or folding back a corner to allow the steam to escape.

1. Place the sausage, ham, green pepper, onion, garlic, chili and olive oil in a large casserole or deep bowl. Stir to coat all the ingredients in oil and cover the bowl loosely.

2. Cook for 6-7 minutes or until the onion and pepper are almost tender.

3. Mix the canned tomatoes, tomato paste and white wine or lemon juice and add to the bowl.

Add the marjoram, bay leaf, grated nutmeg, salt and pepper and loosely cover the bowl.

4. Cook for 2-3 minutes on HIGH, and add the shrimp, tomatoes and rice. Re-cover the bowl and cook for a further 4 minutes, or until all the ingredients are hot. Remove the bay leaf before serving.

Cook's Notes

 TIME: Preparation takes about 20 minutes, and cooking takes 14-17 minutes.

COOK'S TIP: Rice can be cooked successfully in the microwave oven for 12-15 minutes on HIGH in liquid. Leave to stand for 5 minutes covered, stirring occasionally.

VARIATION: Chicken can be used instead of the ham; cut it into 1-inch pieces and cook with the onion and pepper. Salami or garlic sausage can be substituted for the Pepperoni or Merguez.

SHRIMP AND TAMARIND

SERVES 4

*Tamarind has an exotic sweet-sour taste that goes very well
with shrimp and combines perfectly with the spices and chilies
in this sauce.*

2lbs large shrimp
2 tbsps butter or margarine
4 shallots, finely chopped
1 tbsp ground coriander
4 crushed cardamoms
2 tsps turmeric
Pinch nutmeg
1 green chili, seeded and shredded
1 pimento, shredded
Juice of 1 lime
1 tbsp sugar
1 tbsp tamarind extract
¾ cup natural yogurt
Salt and pepper

Step 1 Peel the shrimp and use a toothpick or skewer to remove the black veins.

1. Peel and devein the shrimp and set aside.

2. Heat a browning dish according to the manufacturer's directions. Add the butter or margarine and shallots and cook for 2 minutes on HIGH.

3. Add the spices and shrimp and cook for 1-2 minutes on HIGH.

4. Pour into a casserole and add the chili, pimento,

Step 3 Combine the spices and shrimp in a browning dish and cook briefly.

Step 5 Stir the yogurt into the sauce before leaving it to stand.

lime juice, sugar and tamarind. Stir well and cook for 2 minutes on HIGH.

5. Stir in the yogurt and salt and pepper and leave to stand for 3 minutes before serving.

Cook's Notes

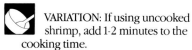

TIME: Preparation takes about 20 minutes, and cooking takes 5-6 minutes plus 3 minutes standing time.

VARIATION: If using uncooked shrimp, add 1-2 minutes to the cooking time.

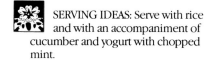

SERVING IDEAS: Serve with rice and with an accompaniment of cucumber and yogurt with chopped mint.

MALABARI FISH

SERVES 4

Fish curries are unusual, at least to Western palates, and this one is rather special. It has a spicy-rich coconut flavored sauce with the addition of pineapple, raisins and almonds.

4 tbsps shredded coconut
½ cup water
4 tbsps oil
1 onion, finely chopped
½ tsp each ground cinnamon, nutmeg, cumin, coriander, turmeric and chili powder
Pinch ground cloves
6 cardamoms
1 bay leaf
1 tsp grated fresh ginger
1 clove garlic, crushed
1lb whitefish, skinned, boned and cut into 2-inch pieces
8oz canned pineapple chunks and juice
1 tbsp chopped coriander leaves
1-2 green chilies, seeded and finely chopped
Pinch salt and pepper
1 tbsp cornstarch
1 tbsp blanched almonds
1 tbsp raisins
½ cup natural yogurt

Step 5 Strain the infused coconut, mix the liquid with the cornstarch and stir it into the fish.

Step 6 Add the pineapple, almonds, raisins and yogurt and mix together well. Leave to stand.

1. Place the coconut and water in a dish and heat for 30 seconds on HIGH. Leave to infuse.

2. Place the oil in a casserole and add the onion. Cover and cook for 2 minutes on HIGH.

3. Add all the spices, the bay leaf, ginger and garlic and heat for 2 minutes on HIGH.

4. Add the fish and strained juice from the pineapple. Add the coriander, chilies, salt and pepper. Cover and cook for 6 minutes on HIGH.

5. Remove the fish and keep it warm. Strain the coconut and mix the liquid with the cornstarch. Stir into the sauce and cook for a further 2-3 minutes on HIGH, stirring carefully, or until it thickens and clears.

6. Return the fish to the sauce and add the pineapple, almonds, raisins and yogurt. Cover and leave to stand for 3-5 minutes before serving. Remove the bay leaf.

Cook's Notes

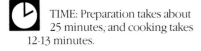 TIME: Preparation takes about 25 minutes; and cooking takes 12-13 minutes.

 PREPARATION: Even though microwave ovens reheat food well, fish dishes are best prepared just before serving.

 COOK'S TIP: Whenever infused liquid is called for in a recipe, use the microwave oven to speed up the process.

SHRIMP AND ZUCCHINI
SERVES 4

Indian cuisine often combines aromatic spices with fiery chilies to set the taste buds tingling.

1lb large shrimp
2 tbsps oil
1 tsp paprika
½ tsp turmeric
1½ tsps ground cumin
Grated fresh ginger
1 clove garlic, crushed
1 red chili, seeded and shredded
2 zucchini, cut in matchsticks
7oz canned tomatoes, crushed
1 bay leaf
2-3 tsps cornstarch mixed with 3 tbsps lemon juice
Salt and pepper

Step 4 Add the shrimp and cook briefly. Cover the bowl tightly and set aside to finish cooking.

Step 3 Combine the vegetables, bay leaf, cornstarch with lemon juice and seasoning. Cook for 5 minutes or until the sauce thickens.

1. Shell and devein the shrimp.

2. Pour the oil into a casserole and add the spices, ginger, garlic and chili. Cook for 2 minutes on HIGH.

3. Add the zucchini, tomatoes, bay leaf, the cornstarch mixed with lemon juice and salt and pepper. Cook on HIGH for 5 minutes.

4. Add the shrimp and cook for 2 minutes on HIGH then leave to stand for 5 minutes to finish cooking. Remove the bay leaf.

Cook's Notes

TIME: Preparation takes about 25 minutes, and cooking takes 9 minutes, plus 5 minutes standing time.

SERVING IDEAS: Serve with plain boiled rice or rice pilaff. Accompany with mango chutney and yogurt.

PREPARATION: During standing time, the food continues to cook in its own heat. Ingredients that only need reheating can be added at this time.

WATCHPOINT: When cooking seafood in a microwave oven, be careful not to overcook as it quickly toughens.

TUNA AU POIVRE

SERVES 4

Green peppercorns lend a sophisticated but spicy taste to tuna.
Brandy and sour cream make this dish extra special.

4 6oz tuna steaks
1 tbsp oil
2 tbsps green peppercorns
1 tbsp brandy
6 tbsps crème fraîche or sour cream
Pinch salt

1. Brush the tuna steaks on both sides with the oil. Crush the peppercorns using a pestle and mortar or a rolling pin and press them onto one side of the tuna steaks.

2. Preheat a browning dish to the maximum time the manufacturer allows and then immediately add the tuna steaks, peppercorn side up.

3. Cook, uncovered, for 7 minutes on HIGH. Cook for an additional 1 minute if the fish does not flake easily when tested.

4. When the fish steaks are done, remove them to a serving dish and keep them warm.

5. Add the brandy to the browning dish and heat for 30 seconds on HIGH.

6. Stir the cream into the juices remaining in the dish and add a pinch of salt to taste. Spoon the sauce over the tuna steaks and serve immediately.

Step 1 Press crushed peppercorns onto one side of the tuna steaks.

Step 2 Put the steaks into a preheated browning dish.

Step 6 To make the sauce, stir the cream into the juices in the browning dish.

Cook's Notes

TIME: Preparation takes about 5 minutes, and cooking takes 10-11 minutes. Browning dishes need preheating.

VARIATION: Use mixed peppercorns, black, green, white and pink, for an attractive effect. If desired, the cream can be omitted.

SERVING IDEAS: Serve with lightly-cooked vegetables such as snow peas, green beans or zucchini.

LIME AND CHILI CHICKEN

SERVES 4

Branding with hot skewers gives microwaved chicken a "barbecued" look. Chilies and limes give it a distinctive taste.

4 boneless chicken breasts
2 limes
1 green chili pepper
Pinch sugar
Salt and pepper
6 tbsps heavy cream

Step 4 Place the chicken in a casserole with sugar, chili, salt, pepper and lime juice.

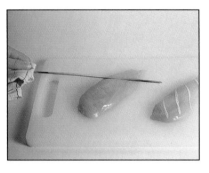

Step 2 Skin the chicken breasts and brand with hot skewers to make a pattern.

Step 6 Stir the cream into the juices in the casserole.

1. Heat 2 metal skewers in a gas flame or on an electric burner.

2. Skin the chicken breasts and make a pattern on the flesh with the hot skewers.

3. Squeeze 1 lime for juice. Peel and slice the other lime thinly. Remove the seeds from the chili pepper and slice it very thinly.

4. Put the chicken into a casserole. Sprinkle over a pinch of sugar, the sliced chili pepper, salt, pepper and lime juice.

5. Cover and cook for 10 minutes on MEDIUM. Remove the chicken and keep warm.

6. Stir the cream into the juices in the casserole. Cook for 2 minutes on HIGH, stirring frequently. Pour over the chicken and garnish with the sliced lime.

Cook's Notes

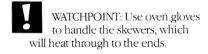

TIME: Preparation takes about 20 minutes, and cooking takes about 12 minutes.

PREPARATION: The skewers take about 15 minutes to become hot enough to sear the chicken. Aluminum skewers will melt in the heat, so use stainless steel. Do not put skewers into the microwave oven.

WATCHPOINT: Use oven gloves to handle the skewers, which will heat through to the ends.

SPICY TOMATO CHICKEN
SERVES 4

Worcestershire sauce provides the hotness in this barbecue-type tomato sauce. It's a perfect way to spice up chicken.

4 chicken breasts, skinned and boned
¼ cup chicken stock or water
1lb canned tomatoes
2 tbsps Worcestershire sauce
1 clove garlic, crushed
2 tbsps tomato paste
2 tbsps cider vinegar
2 tbsps light brown sugar or honey
1 small onion, finely chopped
1 bay leaf
Pinch allspice
Salt and pepper
4 tomatoes, skinned, seeded and cut into thin strips
    to garnish

Step 3 Cook the sauce uncovered to reduce it.

Step 4 In a food processor, blend the sauce until smooth.

Step 1 Place the chicken in one layer in a large casserole, cover and cook until white and opaque.

1. Place the chicken in one layer in a large casserole with the stock or water. Cover tightly and cook on MEDIUM for 10 minutes. Leave to stand, covered, for at least 5 minutes while preparing the sauce.

2. Combine all the sauce ingredients with the cooking liquid from the chicken in a deep bowl.

3. Cook, uncovered, for 7 minutes on HIGH, until the sauce reduces and thickens.

4. Remove the bay leaf and blend the sauce in a food processor until smooth.

5. Arrange the chicken breasts on a serving plate and coat with the sauce. Add the tomato strips and reheat for 30 seconds on HIGH before serving.

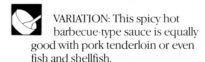

Cook's Notes

TIME: Preparation takes about 15 minutes, and cooking takes about 17 minutes plus 5 minutes standing time.

VARIATION: This spicy hot barbecue-type sauce is equally good with pork tenderloin or even fish and shellfish.

SERVING IDEAS: Rice or pasta are good accompaniments together with a green salad. Corn on the cob makes another good accompaniment.

TANDOORI GUINEA FOWL

SERVES 4

*This marinade gives color and flavor to the guinea fowl and turns
your microwave into an Indian "tandoor," or oven.*

4 Guinea fowl

Marinade
1 small onion, chopped
1 small piece fresh ginger, grated
2 tsps ground coriander
2 tsps ground cumin
2 tsps paprika
1 tsp turmeric
1 tsp chili powder
1 cup plain yogurt
Juice of 1 lime
2 green chili peppers, seeded and chopped
2 tbsps chopped fresh chives
Salt and pepper

To Serve
1 head of lettuce, broken into leaves
4 tomatoes, cut in wedges
1 lemon, cut in wedges

1. Combine all the marinade ingredients together.
Skin the fowl and cut them in half. Prick the flesh and
rub in the marinade. Leave for 1 hour.

2. Cook on HIGH for 20 minutes or until juices
run clear, basting frequently with the marinade.

3. Leave to stand, loosely covered, for 5 minutes
before serving.

4. Heat any remaining marinade on MEDIUM for
1 minute, but do not allow to boil.

5. Pour over the chicken and serve on a bed of
lettuce with tomato and lemon wedges.

Step 1 Prick the skin
of the fowl and rub in
the marinade.

Step 2 Baste or brush
frequently with the
marinade while
cooking.

Cook's Notes

TIME: Preparation takes about
20 minutes plus 1 hour to
marinate the fowl. Cooking takes
about 15 minutes.

COOK'S TIP: A spicy, colorful
coating such as this gives
microwave-cooked chicken a more
appetizing appearance.

BUYING GUIDE: Guinea fowl
are available from butchers and
supermarkets. Chicken portions may
be substituted, if necessary.

LEMON CHICKEN
SERVES 4

This Oriental dish has a fresh-tasting lemony sauce with red pepper flakes providing just the right amount of hotness.

4 chicken breasts, skinned, boned and cut into thin strips

Marinade
4 tbsps soy sauce
2 tsps dry sherry or shao-hsing wine
Salt and pepper

Sauce
3 tbsps salted black beans
2 tbsps water
6 tbsps lemon juice
1 cup chicken stock
4 tbsps sugar
1 tsp sesame oil
3 tbsps cornstarch
2 cloves garlic, finely chopped
¼ tsp red pepper flakes

Lemon slices to garnish

1. Mix chicken with the marinade ingredients, cover and refrigerate for 30 minutes.

2. Crush the black beans, combine with the water and leave to stand until ready to use.

3. Combine remaining sauce ingredients in a shallow dish. Add the chicken, marinade and black beans, cover and cook on HIGH for 7-9 minutes,

Step 2 Crush the black beans into the water and leave to soak.

Step 3 Combine all the sauce ingredients with the chicken, marinade and black beans.

stirring halfway through the cooking time.

4. Once the cornstarch has cleared, leave the chicken to stand, covered, for 2 minutes before serving. Garnish with lemon slices.

Cook's Notes

TIME: Preparation takes about 30 minutes. Cooking takes 7-9 minutes plus 2 minutes standing time.

SERVING IDEAS: Serve with either plain boiled rice or fried rice.

WATCHPOINT: Because the seeds are included in dried red peppers and because the drying process intensifies flavor, red pepper flakes are hotter than fresh chilies.

BUYING GUIDE: Salted beans are available in delicatessens and Chinese grocers. Bottled black bean sauce is available in supermarkets and can be substituted.

CHICKEN VERACRUZ

SERVES 4

This dish is every bit as tasty as it looks. The chili powder makes it spicy and three kinds of peppers make it colorful.

1lb chicken meat, skinned and boned
2 tbsps oil
2 medium onions, diced
2 tsps chili powder
1 clove garlic, crushed
2 tsps dried oregano
2 tsps cumin seed, lightly crushed
1 tsp cayenne pepper
Salt
1 tbsp cornstarch mixed with 2 tbsps water
1 cup chicken stock
8oz canned tomatoes
15oz canned chickpeas, drained and rinsed
1 small red pepper, seeded and diced
1 small green pepper, seeded and diced
1 small yellow pepper, seeded and diced

Step 2 After cooking the onion, add all the other ingredients, except the chickpeas and peppers, and cook until the chicken is tender.

Step 4 Stir in the chickpeas and peppers and finish cooking.

Step 1 Cut the chicken into small cubes.

1. Cut the chicken into small cubes. Place the oil and the onions in a bowl with the chili powder and cook on HIGH for 3 minutes or until the onion softens.

2. Add the chicken and the remaining ingredients except the chickpeas and peppers and stir well. Cover and cook on HIGH for 10 minutes.

3. Turn down to LOW or DEFROST and cook for 20 minutes or until the chicken is tender.

4. Add the chickpeas and peppers and cook for a further 5 minutes on HIGH.

5. Allow to stand for 2 minutes before serving.

Cook's Notes

TIME: Preparation takes about 25 minutes, and cooking takes about 38 minutes plus 2 minutes standing time.

COOK'S TIP: Rinsing canned pulses before using gives them a fresher flavor.

SERVING IDEAS: An avocado salad makes a good accompaniment to this informal supper dish.

DICED CHICKEN AND PEPPERS

SERVES 4

Chinese cooking is quick and so is microwave cooking, so why not combine them in a spicy and colorful chicken dish.

2 tbsps oil
1 clove garlic, minced
1lb chicken meat, skinned, boned and diced
1 small red chili pepper, seeded and diced
1 tsp cornstarch
2 tbsps white wine
2 tbsps soy sauce
4 tbsps chicken stock
2 green peppers, diced
Pinch sugar (optional)
Salt
½ small can bamboo shoots, diced

and stock. Stir well and cover the dish.

4. Cook for 7-9 minutes on HIGH, stirring halfway through the cooking time. Add the green pepper, sugar, if using, and salt if needed.

5. Cook for 30 seconds on HIGH, add bamboo shoots and leave to stand, covered, for 2 minutes before serving.

Step 2 Cook the garlic in the oil, add the chicken and stir to coat.

Step 4 Stir halfway through cooking and add the green pepper and sugar, if using.

Step 5 Add the bamboo shoots, cover and leave to stand.

1. Heat the oil for 30 seconds on HIGH in a large casserole dish.

2. Add the garlic and cook for 30 seconds on HIGH. Add the chicken and stir to coat with oil.

3. Add the chili pepper, cornstarch, wine, soy sauce

Cook's Notes

TIME: Preparation takes about 20 minutes, and cooking takes 8½-10½ minutes plus 2 minutes standing time.

PREPARATION: Chinese cooking, whether done in a wok or in a microwave oven is very quick. It helps to have all the ingredients prepared before beginning to cook.

SERVING IDEAS: Accompany the dish with plain boiled rice, fried rice or Chinese noodles.

EGGPLANT SLICES IN YOGURT

SERVES 4-6

*The Indian influence in this dish is obvious. Methi is a traditional
Indian herb, but coriander is easier to find.*

2 large eggplants, cut into ¼-inch-thick rounds
Salt
3 tbsps oil
1 tsp chili powder
¼ tsp turmeric
1 tsp garam masala
1 green chili, seeded and thinly sliced
½ cup natural yogurt
1 sprig methi or corinader leaves, chopped
Paprika

Step 2 Preheat the oil and then cook the rinsed and dried eggplant slices.

Step 1 Score the eggplant slices and sprinkle them with salt.

1. Lightly score the eggplants on both sides and sprinkle with salt. Leave to stand for 30 minutes, drain and pat dry.

2. Heat the oil in a casserole for 30 seconds on HIGH and stir in the chili powder, turmeric, garam masala, chili and eggplant slices.

3. Cover the dish and cook on HIGH for 2-3 minutes. Pour over the yogurt and leave to stand for 3-5 minutes.

4. Sprinkle over the methi or coriander leaves and the paprika and serve hot or cold.

Cook's Notes

 TIME: Preparation takes about 10 minutes, and cooking takes 2-4 minutes.

 PREPARATION: Eggplants can taste bitter. To remedy this, sprinkle with salt and stand for 30 minutes to draw out the juices. Be sure to rinse well and then pat dry.

SERVING IDEAS: This makes a good starter or side dish.

DAHL

SERVES 4

*Nutritious lentils are a perfect foil for spices. A microwave oven
makes cooking pulses faster and easier.*

1 cup lentils, brown or green
4 tbsps butter or margarine
1 large onion, finely chopped
1 clove garlic, crushed
1 red or green chili pepper, seeded and finely
    chopped
1 tsp each ground cumin, coriander and turmeric
½ tsp each ground cinnamon and nutmeg
3 cups vegetable stock
Salt and pepper
1 bay leaf
Chopped fresh coriander leaves

1. Cover the lentils with water and soak overnight.

Alternatively, microwave for 10 minutes on HIGH to
bring to the boil and then allow the lentils to boil
for 2 minutes. Leave to stand, covered, for 1 hour.

2. Melt the butter or margarine for 1 minute on
HIGH in a large casserole. Add the onion, garlic,
chili pepper and spices. Cook for 4 minutes on
MEDIUM.

3. Drain the lentils and add to the casserole with
the vegetable stock, salt, pepper and bay leaf. Cover
and cook on HIGH for 45 minutes, or until the
lentils are soft and tender.

4. Allow to stand, covered, for 5-10 minutes before
serving. Remove the bay leaf and add the chopped
coriander. If preferred, the dahl can be puréed
before serving.

Step 1 Place the lentils in a bowl and cover them with water. Cover the bowl and microwave to boil the water.

Step 3 Drain the precooked lentils and add them to the other ingedients.

Cook's Notes

TIME: Preparation takes about 25 minutes plus soaking time, which will vary according to method used. Cooking takes about 45 minutes plus 5-10 minutes standing time.

WATCHPOINT: Incompletely cooked pulses can be dangerous to eat. Make sure lentils are soft and properly cooked, according to instructions.

SPICY CUCUMBERS

SERVES 4

This unusual side dish is Chinese in origin. Brief microwave cooking helps intensify the flavors.

1 large cucumber
Salt
3 tbsps light soy sauce
Pinch five-spice powder
¼ tsp red pepper flakes
2 tsps sesame oil
1 tbsp rice vinegar
3 tbsps coriander leaves

1. Peel thin strips off the cucumber for a green and white striped effect.

2. Cut in half lengthwise, or in quarters if the cucumber is thick.

3. Cut each length into 2-inch pieces. Sprinkle with salt and leave to stand for 30 minutes. Wash and dry well.

4. Combine the cucumber with all the remaining ingredients except the coriander in a deep bowl. Partially cover and cook for 2 minutes on HIGH.

5. Add the coriander and leave in the bowl to cool. When cold, refrigerate. Serve on the same day.

Step 3 Sprinkle the cucumber with salt and leave it in a colander to drain either in the sink or on paper towels.

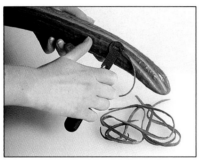

Step 1 Peel thin strips of skin from the cucumber to make stripes.

Step 5 Add the coriander to the warm cucumber and leave to cool in the bowl.

Cook's Notes

TIME: Preparation takes about 30 minutes since the cucumbers must be salted and left to stand. Cooking takes 2 minutes.

COOK'S TIP: Salting cucumbers helps to draw out excess moisture and keeps the dressing from becoming watery. It also makes cucumbers more digestible.

SERVING IDEAS: Serve as a starter to a Chinese meal or as an accompaniment to cold or barbecued meat or poultry.

CURRIED VEGETABLES

SERVES 6-8

The vegetables in this delicious golden sauce can be varied according to season. Even frozen vegetables get a lift from this combination of spices.

1 tbsp oil
1 onion, finely chopped
1 green chili pepper, seeded and finely chopped
1 small piece fresh ginger, grated
2 cloves garlic, crushed
½ tsp ground coriander
½ tsp ground cumin
1 tsp ground turmeric
2 potatoes, peeled and diced
1 eggplant, cut into small cubes
14oz canned tomatoes, drained
1 small cauliflower, cut into flowerets
½ cup vegetable or chicken stock
8oz okra, trimmed and washed
1 cup roasted, unsalted cashews
4 tbsps shredded coconut
4 tbsps natural yogurt

1 minute on HIGH.

3. Add the potatoes, eggplant and tomatoes. Cover loosely and cook on HIGH for 8-10 minutes or until the potatoes and eggplant are almost tende

4. Add the cauliflower, stock and okra. Cover

Step 3 Add the potatoes, eggplant and tomatoes.

Step 2 Stir the spices into the onion, chili, ginger and garlic.

Step 4 Finally add the cauliflower and okra, which need less cooking.

1. Heat the oil in a large bowl or casserole dish for 1 minute on HIGH. Add the onion, chili pepper, ginger and garlic. Cook on HIGH for 1 minute further.

2. Add the spices and cook for an additional

loosely and cook on HIGH for 3-4 minutes, or until the vegetables are almost tender.

5. Add the cashews and the shredded coconut. Add salt and pepper to taste and serve hot, topped with natural yogurt.

Cook's Notes

 TIME: Preparation takes about 25 minutes, and cooking takes 13-16 minutes.

 COOK'S TIP: If the spices are cooked for a minute before adding any liquid, they will lose their harsh raw taste and develop a fuller flavor.

 SERVING IDEAS: Serve as a side dish to a full Indian meal or with grilled meat or poultry. For a vegetarian meal add rice and use vegetable stock.

SWEET-SOUR CABBAGE

SERVES 4

Crisp cabbage gets a sweet and sour taste with the zip of chili pepper
in this oriental relish.

1 medium head white cabbage, about 2lbs
1 small red chili pepper (use less if desired)
½ cup light brown sugar
6 tbsps rice vinegar
2 tbsps light soy sauce
Salt
3 tbsps oil

1. Cut the cabbage into ½-inch slices, discarding the core.

2. Cut the chili pepper into short, thin strips, discarding the seeds.

3. Mix all the ingredients together except the oil.

4. Pour the oil into a large bowl and heat for 2 minutes on HIGH. Add the cabbage mixture and cover the bowl with pierced plastic wrap.

5. Cook on HIGH for 9-11 minutes. Allow to cool in the bowl, stirring frequently. When cold, refrigerate.

Step 1 Cut the cabbage into slices, discarding the core.

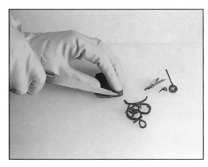

Step 2 Cut the chili into thin strips, discarding the seeds. Wear rubber gloves to handle hot chilies.

Cook's Notes

 TIME: Preparation takes about 20 minutes, and cooking takes 11-13 minutes.

 COOK'S TIP: The cabbage will keep for several days if stored in its liquid in the refrigerator.

 SERVING IDEAS: Serve as a Chinese starter or as a side dish.

ZUCCHINI CURRY

SERVES 4-6

Zucchini are delicious in a spicy tomato sauce. They are especially good cooked in a microwave oven because they keep their color and texture.

1 tbsp oil
1 tsp cumin seed
1 tsp mustard seed
½ tsp chili powder
¼ tsp ground turmeric
8oz canned tomatoes and juice
1 green chili, seeded and finely chopped
8oz zucchini, cut into ¼-inch slices
Salt
1 tbsp cornstarch mixed with 3 tbsps water (optional)

1. Heat the oil for 30 seconds on HIGH and add the cumin seed, mustard seed, chili powder and turmeric. Cook for 1-2 minutes on HIGH.

2. Add the tomatoes and juice, chili pepper and zucchini. Cover and cook on HIGH for 3 minutes.

3. Add salt to taste and leave to stand for 1 minute before serving.

4. If desired, thicken the sauce with the cornstarch and water. Cook for a further 1-2 minutes on HIGH.

Step 1 Add the whole and ground spices to the oil and cook briefly.

Step 2 Add the tomatoes and their juice to the spices together with the chili and zucchini.

Cook's Notes

TIME: Preparation takes about 20 minutes, and cooking takes 4-7 minutes.

PREPARATION: Cooking the cumin seed before adding the other ingredients will develop its flavor and soften the seeds.

SERVING IDEAS: This can be served as a main course for an Indian vegetarian meal or as a side dish with meat or poultry.

CHICKPEAS WITH SPICES

SERVES 4-6

A sunny, spicy dish that is as good cold as it is hot. Serve it on a bed of rice for a vegetarian main course.

2 tbsps oil
1 small onion, finely chopped
1 clove garlic, minced
1 small piece fresh ginger, grated
1 tsp ground coriander
1 tsp chili powder
¼ tsp ground turmeric
4oz canned tomatoes, roughly chopped, plus juice
1 green chili, seeded and chopped
Salt
2 sprigs fresh coriander, chopped
1 bay leaf
15oz canned chickpeas
4 cardamoms
Juice of 1 lemon

Step 2 Make sure the cardamom pods are sufficiently well crushed to release the seeds within.

Step 2 Add the chickpeas with half of their can liquid to the other ingredients.

1. Put the oil in a casserole and add the onion garlic, ginger and ground spices. Cook for 1 minute on HIGH.

Peel the ginger and use the fine side of a grater to produce a purée. Discard any stringy pieces.

2. Add the tomatoes and juice, chili, salt, coriander and bay leaf. Add the chickpeas and half of their liquid, salt, cardamoms and lemon juice and cover the casserole.

3. Cook on HIGH for 4-6 minutes or until completely heated through. Remove the bay leaf before serving.

Cook's Notes

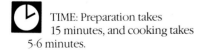 TIME: Preparation takes 15 minutes, and cooking takes 5-6 minutes.

VARIATION: Fresh tomatoes may be used instead of canned ones. Use about 8oz peeled and seeded tomatoes, roughly chopped. Water or stock may be necessary if using fresh tomatoes.

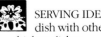 SERVING IDEAS: Serve as a side dish with other curries or with chicken dishes.

Index

Edited by Jane Adams and Jillian Stewart
Photographed by Peter Barry
Recipes Prepared and Styled for Photography by Bridgeen Deery
and Wendy Devenish
Designed by Claire Leighton, Sally Strugnell and Alison Jewell